7

Secret Sources

of Inspiration:

A Snappy Guide for

Creative Procrastinators

ALEXEI AULD

While every precaution has been taken in the preparation of this book, the publisher assumes no responsibility for errors or omissions, or for damages resulting from the use of the information contained herein.

7 SECRET SOURCES OF INSPIRATION: A SNAPPY GUIDE FOR CREATIVE PROCRASTINATORS

First edition. April 24, 2016.

ISBN: 979-8989457212

Written by Alexei Auld.

Table of Contents

A STROKE LEFT ME PARALYZED AND SPEECHLESS.

This was not supposed to happen. I was young and in great health.

But there I was. Hospitalized. Haunted by my deferred dreams. Drafts of books and screenplays scattered through my head, on paper, and my computer. My handwriting was horrid, so who could decipher it? And my computer files? How would my wife or anyone know which stories were just an edit away from publishing? And my best stories were skeletal drafts scribbled in indecipherable chicken scratch in my apartment. My completed works would continue collecting digital dust and remain trapped in the computer, like my unfinished works, in my useless shell.

I'd spent my life delaying the creative call. I always thought I'd have time to write at some later date. And it always was later. After college. After law school. After making partner. Maybe retirement? At some point, I'd do it because I had time.

But my time had run out.

I made a vow that if I made it out of the hospital, I would be done with the self-doubt. I would let the world know that I existed. The stories I needed to tell would be preserved and passed on.

Intact. Pure. Authentic.

My experience is what motivates me to create.

As for you?

I don't know you. I have no clue what your story is or what stories you lie within you.

But know this.

If you go to your grave without expressing yourself, you will deprive future generations of benefitting from your life experiences, your stories, and your perspective.

And that would be a shame.

Especially as we are living in a time where the ability to create and share your work has never been easier.

You just need some motivation.

This book will demonstrate why this is the best time for your creative expression. Hopefully you will be inspired to not allow obstacles like gatekeepers or your own perceived limitations prevent you from taking advantage of the creative production, distribution, and marketing tools that are waiting to be used by you to spread your creative vision. I will show you how to leverage your life experiences and preserve your perspective through expressive solutions.

The specific tools vary on the project and, in this exciting world, may be replaced by innovations created after this book is published. Feel free to visit auldsolutions.com and/or drop me a line if you'd like specific information on what is best for your project.

You are here now. But there will come a time when you will be gone. Take the steps to transform your thoughts from the temporal to the eternal.

GATEKEEPERS

When my father attended college in the 1960s, he had a popular comic strip in his university student paper about Anansi the Spider. For those who don't know, stories of the folk character originated with the Ashanti in West Africa (what is now referred to as Ghana). Anansi stories spread throughout the world, including the West Indies, Suriname, Sierra Leone, and the Netherlands Antilles. On Curaçao, Aruba, and Bonaire, he is known as Nanzi. In South Carolina, Anansi was known as "Aunt Nancy."

After graduation, my father was ready to take on the world with his comic strip. He scheduled an interview with the nation's largest comic syndication company. Success was at his fingertips.

During the meeting, the representative lavished my father's comic strip with praise.

But rejected it.

The reason?

The characters were African.

"Great for New York and DC, bad for the rest of the country. Sorry, son."

My father gathered his things and went home.

He eventually had the comic strip published in other countries, but never had access to the US market. Without a syndicate or a major publisher behind him, he and many other creatives were shut out of the system.

* * *

Gatekeepers exist to identify which projects are worthy of a corporate investment. They don't have the best track records, since no one knows which project will resonate with a mass audience. And at the end of the day, that's what it's about: the biggest audience possible. If you do not already have an audience, are too old, don't look like an all-American underwear model, or remind them of themselves, you are unlikely to receive the full marketing heft of the corporations gatekeepers represent.

And their jobs are on the line, so good luck finding one to take a chance on you.

In the past, tremendous financial resources were required to manifest creative projects. In addition, there was limited access to distribution sources to get those projects to consumers.

Digital innovation changed that.

If my father graduated from college fifty years later, with advances in technology and opened pathways to distribution, he wouldn't have had to waste his time and money seeking gatekeeper approval. He would have a means to spread his work worldwide without asking for permission.

And now, you have access to tools to create books, video content, and music recordings at the lowest cost since the cavemen created rock art.

Better yet? You have access to the same distribution sources as the gatekeepers. Your books, music, and video works share the same digital shelf space without under-the-table payments.

This is an unprecedented opportunity to spread your voice and creative vision to the world at reduced costs. With no gatekeeper approval necessary.

If you want help, you can get it and be the boss. You decide when your work is done. You have control with no filter. No one diluting your vision. No one undermining your perspective.

CONTROL YOUR NARRATIVE

If you die without telling your story, you have one hope.

That someone will tell it for you.

It could be a friend or family member. Or even a stranger. Who knows whether or not they share your agenda or care about authenticity?

My message to you is straightforward:

Control your narrative

You are still here to finish your stories. And the beauty of it all? You don't need to please any gatekeepers. You can hire your own editors. Hire your own cover artist. Decide for yourself when it's ready. And release it instead of waiting for permission.

Your work doesn't need to die with you. And better yet? You don't need it gathering cobwebs until someone dusts it off and finishes it without you.

WHO BETTER THAN YOU?

People get too caught up in perfection. Unpublished writers rewriting their drafts into oblivion. Fixating on character names. Fidgeting with lighting.

The goal is to produce.

Create. Publish. Move on.

Your work is perfection. A perfect representation of you at a particular stage of your life.

Does everyone laugh at every single joke you make? Does your retelling of experiences you find fascinating enrapture everyone? Are you in entertainment bliss viewing every officially produced movie, book, artwork, or television show?

Of course not.

Stop holding yourself to an impossible standard.

For books, get a proofreader and publish.

For shows, make corrections in the next edition.

For artwork, don't bother asking.

And please don't go back after you've released it to the world. You see a mistake? Unless it's a printing error, glitch, or some technical difficulty, move on.

Unless you only have that one book/show/artwork in you.

But if you have more to say, say it before you end up in a position where you are no longer able to express yourself.

FROM CONSUMER TO PRODUCER

I spent most of my life as miserable consumer. Suffering under the stories of others. Reading experiences that ignored my own. Seething at ceremonies that rewarded recycled reinforcement of the status quo. I was waiting for someone to finally tell a story I could get behind. And raging when, once again, "my story" was a fleeting footnote of a larger narrative with a questionable political and cultural agenda.

I decided to transition my existence as a CONSUMER of content to a PRODUCER of my point of view.

And that transition has enabled me to exorcize personal demons by sheer virtue of writing and publishing. That's right, exorcised, without priests, holy water, or (warning, dated reference) throwing up split-pea soup.

You have at least one story to tell. One creative project. You might have felt motivated watching some horrid but critically acclaimed movie. Wasted time on a novel you knew you should've stopped reading a few pages after you started. Listened to some garbage on the radio that passed for music. And what did you do? You told yourself you could do better.

But you didn't.

Instead, you moved on to some other form of entertainment and ignored the call to create.

At some point, you probably heard someone fudge history, intentionally or unintentionally. It might have been some story in your past or situation that occurred. And your perspective wasn't considered. You might have added your two cents, but what about those who didn't have the benefit of being there to hear your take? Think about how many stories or situations have passed with a verbal correction. Now think about all the stories and situations involving you, someone you love, or some issue you care about, which occurred behind your back. Where was your perspective?

You probably told yourself "One day, when the time is right, I'm going to..."

The time is right now.

Stop waiting for your unpublished opinions to be discovered. In fact, stop discovering others while you wantonly wallow in POV purgatory. Create your own opportunity and worry about discovery later. Be a producer and save your consumption for entertainment, inspirational, and enlightenment value. Hopefully all three at the same time.

PERFECTION: A CAUTIONARY TALE

You might think the time isn't ripe yet for your first, or next, creative project. You have other things on your plate, like work, home renovation, grocery shopping. I get it.

But do you?

In college, a childhood friend and I spoke about growing up in DC before helicopter parenting, the crack epidemic, and gentrification.

I felt inspired to write a book.

He frowned. "But that's my book."

I said, "Maybe we can work on it together?"

He agreed. It needed more than just an idea. It needed historical context. So I set out doing research. Hours at the National Archives. Days at scattered libraries across the DC-MD-VA region. I even convinced a professor to overlook the project. When it came time to write, I approached my friend.

He wasn't ready.

It was the story he wanted to tell and it was personal to him. My professor said that it wasn't worth ruining a friendship. I agreed.

Twenty-five years later, the book remains unwritten.

We're no longer friends—not that there was a blowup; our lives just moved in different directions. Not that my friend has moved on from the project.

Emotionally speaking, that is.

I spoke to him a year ago after visiting home. He complained about other projects that "got the story wrong." Projects ranging from books to live-action fiction movies. His rage was visceral. Replete with popping veins, flushed skin, and the dreaded lip snarl.

He knew all the details about similar projects. Similar *completed* projects.

I suggested he finish his book we tried starting twenty-five years ago. With the tools available, he could put something together with a minimal budget.

"I don't have time for that."

I suggested he write a guide showing the errors in the projects, so he could at least do something with all his knowledge.

"I don't have time for that."

What about filming a short series on his smartphone or computer webcam? He could just record what he told me and put it on YouTube.

"I don't have time for that."

He had the time to tell me, but no time to record himself telling me?

I realized his problem: He wasn't a creator; he was a complainer.

And for him, that's enough. It's unlikely he'll do anything but feast on anger. And have nothing to show for his meal.

As for me? I moved on with other projects and lost interest in resuscitating one that died twenty-five years ago. Projects of my own that don't require an emotional roadblock I can't remove.

DON'T PSYCH YOURSELF OUT

When my screenplay *Moving Picks* was accepted for a Sundance writing workshop, I was pumped. I envisioned leaving my job and becoming a full-time writer.

Until I found out the paths that others took.

"You can't make it in NY. You need to be in LA."

Being in LA meant practicing law in California, which meant taking the bar exam again. Given my bar prep experience parodied in the Chumped series, I wasn't about to commit to that. But I wanted to keep an open mind.

I asked, "Where do I work?"

"At 7-11."

I told myself I could do it. And asked, "How long do I have to work there?"

"Until you get discovered."

My cousin, who enjoyed a successful career as an Emmy-winning producer, told me the same thing.

"You need to be in LA."

I thought New York had a film industry.

"It does, but everything is who you know. You have to be able to take a meeting within minutes."

7-11? Making slushie drinks? Working minimum wage while carrying six-figure law school debt? How would that work into my ten-year repayment plan?

Didn't seem good to me. So I put that dream on hold.

Maybe life as a filmmaker and not a writer?

I attended a panel where industry insiders told me that it takes ten years from script to screen...

If I was lucky.

"And for screenplays about minorities that don't involve drug addiction? You'd need a lot of luck."

Let me break something down to you. I was two years out of law school. Most people who go to law school are risk averse. Going to med school and being a doctor? What if you kill a patient? Going to business school and running your own company? What if your business fails?

So we go to law school. Where we learn from the worst-case scenarios.

Literally.

The cases are fraught with peril. Legal horror stories where the simplest actions result in death and dismemberment. So if you weren't risk averse going in, you sure as hell were coming out.

I didn't want to go to film school and accrue more debt, so I took a famous DIY class with A-list independent directors as alums.

"Money. You need to ask for money to shoot your films."

Where?

"Dentists. High income, low prestige. Or better yet, convince folks that they should spend ten grand on your film project, instead of a weekend cocaine binge in Vegas."

My risk aversion killed it.

"Or ask family members and friends."

Sounded good, until I realized that films rarely make a return on their investment. So I'd be asking for money I knew would never be repaid. No one in my family had that kind of money to waste. And I felt guilty convincing them otherwise.

So I gave up on my screenplays and my Hollywood dreams.

Until I discovered reverse optioning.

The audiences I sought didn't read screenplays.

They read books.

Access to content creation was easier. I didn't need to raise tens of thousands of dollars. And my stories would be memorialized in a more accessible format. And if I, or any of my readers, cared enough, a film adaptation would follow at later date.

My journey was more complicated at the time because the tools weren't available.

Fortunately, the tools are available now. I've taken advantage and reach audiences in stores, online, and in classrooms where my books are required reading.

All the tools are available for anyone, but the biggest obstacle remains.

Inactivity.

For many reasons, we stymie our creativity. Instead of being active, we're passive. And it doesn't have to be that way. Sometimes, we just need a little inspiration and hope that it can be done.

STOP SEEKING CORPORATE VALIDATION

Life would be easier if you had the full heft of a corporate marketing machine behind you.

In the past, you had no choice but to waste precious creative time chasing it.

But not all that glitters is gold.

A musician who received frequent rejections from major record labels decided to do his own thing. He made his own recordings and worked hard to garner a devoted following. Within a few years, he had success on the college radio circuit. Success that attracted three of the five major labels. After signing the deal, he lost all control of his career. The label selected the producer, his musical direction, and release schedule. Within the span of a year, each of his label point people left or were fired. Without the people who brought him in, he felt unwanted. He asked if he could go on tour to make some money, and the label rejected his request. They had a release schedule with which he was contractually obligated to oblige. They ended up re-recording his independently produced hits and giving him a duet with a bestselling singer. His record was released, received acclaim, and he felt hollow.

He'd lost all control of his career.

He wanted to put out new material, but the label didn't think it was time, despite his previously successful independent schedule.

Touring wasn't fun anymore. The money wasn't enough to make things better. Technology had improved, so he recorded an album on his own, just to test it out. He knew better than release it, lest he breach his contract. He played the newly recorded material to friends, and they agreed the quality was better than what he'd recorded with a bigger budget and label backing.

He knew it was time to move on and do his own thing.

He sought a release from the label, as his seventh label representative had been fired. After months of negotiation, he received his release.

He now has freedom. Technology enabled him to put out a quality product.

And he reaped the financial, creative, and psychological rewards.

TALK IS CHEAP

So many people talk about what they're going to do. And once people realize you are a creative visionary, they might scoff and suggest they have stories just as good, if not better, than yours.

The fact is, all they'll do is talk about doing. Without doing. They'll crap on people who are getting the job done. The reality is, once they die, so will their unmemorialized opinions.

Don't have an unmemoralized opinion.

Give life to your opinion. Make your experiences immortal. Create art. Whether it is a poem. A memoir. A short story. A YouTube video. Make your presence known by recording and releasing it. In doing so, you will separate yourself from the watchers. The complainers. Those who said "what if."

And you will become a "what is."

DISCOVER YOURSELF

Lin-Manuel Miranda wanted a career in musical theatre. As a Latino actor, there were only three big roles available. One of them, *Man of La Mancha*, was out of the question because he didn't have the pipes. Instead of giving up, he created a musical, *The Heights*, which accomplished many goals:

- Validated his experience growing up in Washington Heights

- Created a customized musical leading-man opportunity

- Provided a platform that created other opportunities

Miranda didn't just create a one-man play, he expanded his vision and created opportunity for other Latino actors who probably faced the same stereotyped casting struggles. Additionally, the success of *The Heights* enabled him to break more barriers, including creating *Hamilton*, where he stars as Alexander Hamilton in a unique historical hip-hop interpretation with diverse casting.

Unlike the average response of simply hating on limited opportunities by narrow casting, he did something about it.

If you lack the resources, do a one-person show. Want to expand your audience? Put it online.

LEVERAGE YOUR RESOURCES

African-American artists in Washington, DC faced a yearly challenge from galleries and museums.

Black History Month.

It was the only month in the year that the galleries and museums wanted to exhibit black artists. The problem?

African-American artists wouldn't have any display opportunities for the remaining eleven months. As insulting as it was that blacks could only be publicly acknowledged as artists one month a year, competition was fierce for the few slots in February. To make matters worse, some galleries insisted artists pay them fifty percent of all revenue from artwork sold anywhere in a fifty-mile radius of DC, regardless of where the work was exhibited.

In other words, if in October you sold your work to someone who didn't even attend the February exhibition, you still owed fifty percent of that sale to the gallery.

And this was when Washington, DC was a predominantly black city.

Double dip in frustration.

One artist decided to open his own space. After a few successful years, the rent was just too damn high.

So he realized he had another venue.

His backyard.

He staged barbecues and art exhibitions for friends, family, and collectors.

And sold more work than ever before by leveraging his community.

A similar venue challenge led a musician to use her church as a staging place. Friends, family, and parishioners flocked to her concerts. And her church members used their relationships with other branches throughout the area for other concerts. Some members in other cities had contacts with bigger venues when the church wasn't large enough. She ended up receiving mainstream visibility and success.

These stories of independent entrepreneurial spirit producing results are many. View obstacles as creative challenges. Tap into that same source which enables you to produce something from nothing to manifest your vision. Leverage your community and resources you may not be aware that you have. Record it, put it online, and share with the world.

EXPERIENTIAL INSPIRATIONS

- I hated studying for the New York bar exam. It was a lonely, isolating experience, and some of the lessons weren't sticking. I knew there had to be a better way than rote memorization. For some reason, I remembered the time in kindergarten when I learned fire safety. A firefighter came into our class and taught us the "Stop, Drop, and Roll" method. He described the process, demonstrated it, and required each and every one of us to do it. And it stuck. Looking back, I wondered what would happen if someone who had a hard time memorizing the law had to break it to internalize it? I jotted down some notes and went back to studying. After taking the bar exam, the lessons remained...and so did my notes. I wrote a screenplay called *Mens Rea* and later turned it into *Chumped Vol 3: Cease to Persist*.

- Complaints about abuse and mistreatment of Native Americans on film sets made me wonder what would happen if there actually was something more sinister afoot. I wrote *Luscious Melchus 3: Picture Show Wendigo* as an extreme example of life as a Hollywood Indian.

- Working an eighteen-hour job made me long for my younger days of getting away with doing absolutely nothing. I remembered watching professional wrestling, specifically the old gimmick where a wrestler would fake an injury and take advantage of in-ring confusion by switching places with another wrestler who wore an identical mask. I wondered if that would work in real life: having a masked man take my place at work while I went on vacation. I later turned it into *Chumped Vol 2: Beating in Progress.*

- During my time in the hospital, I thought about the faith we put in doctors and nurses to take care of us. But how do we know they actually have our best interests at heart? What if there was something more sinister afoot? I took notes and later turned it into *Llorona*.

EXPRESS YOURSELF

In law school, I saw *The Replacement Killers* with some friends who loved Asian action flicks. If you count my Chinese-Jamaican ancestry, you could say all of us were Asian.

The movie featured Hong Kong megastar Chow Yun-fat and Mira Sorvino. It served its purpose of proving an escape from the monotony of schoolwork. It wasn't the best movie I'd seen, but I got my money's worth. After the credits rolled, I realized the difference between having heritage and being ethnic.

My friends left the theatre pissed.

"Man."

"Same old crap."

I didn't get it. Movie seemed fine enough.

"You don't get it, Alexei. They didn't kiss."

"Mira and Chow?"

"Yup. He kicks ass, but doesn't get the girl."

Another friend piped up: "We never get the girl."

"How many times have you seen an Asian guy kiss someone in TV or film?"

I had never thought about it before. Once I did, I compared Asian leads in American productions versus Asian film and television productions.

In US films, ass kicking wasn't accompanied by lip kissing. The Asian hero would overcome all obstacles in his way. Save the damsel in distress. And get a passionate, heartfelt...

Pat on the back.

I felt pissed off and created playboy lawyer Rufus Wang in a screenplay...where he received a hell of a lot more than a pat on the back. After turning the screenplay into the book *Chumped*, I gave Rufus his own story in *Billionaire Secrets of a Wanglorious Bastard*. Will it ever be turned into a movie? Time will tell.

The lesson here is that my anger and frustration was a catalyst for change. I could have remained angry at the inequity and waited for media with an Asian romantic lead, and even longer for a Chinese-Jamercian one, to come along.

But I didn't.

Instead, I did it myself.

You might feel the same when reflecting on the classics. Whether it was embarrassment you felt in school when reading Mark Twain's rendering of Nigger Jim and Injun Joe, or watching another helpless princess rescued by some dude. You don't want future generations to feel the shame you felt.

So why not help them?

Take those public domain stories and write one of your own from the perspective of Jim, Joe, or Sleeping Beauty. Or do a *Pride and Prejudice and Zombies* by combining a classic with a modern genre.

Or better yet, create your own characters and worlds.

DON'T FEED THE GATEKEEPING TROLLS

Not all gatekeepers are on a corporate payroll.

Some of them can be your friends and family.

If there is something you need to express and try to share your vision and excitement, whether mild or extreme, with your closest friends and family...

THEY CRAP ON IT.

Their tactics vary from obvious patronizing to out-and-out hostility. It's one thing to have people who have done it before trying to get rid of competition; it's quite another to have people who don't have a creative bone in their body trying to humiliate you for yours.

Instead of creating something eternal, they want you to do absolutely nothing, just like them. They don't understand your creative yearning because they either never had one, or killed it long ago.

And now they want to kill yours. Like vampires, they feed on your pain.

You could listen, but what will you be doing instead? Sitting on your butt consuming other people's work?

* * *

I was one of six screenwriters invited to an exclusive networking event with film industry gatekeepers. Instead of inspiration, we received depression. The gatekeepers told us a miniscule number of projects get green-lit for production. And a smaller number would actually make it to screen. The hurdles were unpredictable, especially for non-mainstream projects. They regaled us with soul-crushing stories and explicitly told us to not waste our time with non-mainstream projects that won't ever be viewed in theaters.

A friend said, "But it's just a screen."

A gatekeeper tittered. "You need relationships with the companies that own them. Relationships that you don't have."

Instead of giving up, my friend replied with a means his cousin used to stage events back home. Another friend expanded that idea with how she did something similar on the rez. Someone else added another ingredient to the mix...

And on the spot, we created a way to display films at reduced cost to rural audiences.

With our own resources.

Without gatekeepers.

"What about the mainstream?"

Our films weren't for the mainstream.

"How can you make a profit?"

One of my peers noted the sold-out crowds he experienced through an alternate screening model that worked in his state. He knew the audience. Had access to them.

The gatekeeper scoffed. "How much money are you talking about?"

The per-show figure made the gatekeeper blush. His friends gasped.

We turned our backs to them and continued the plan. We created a new model of distribution. And we didn't need them to execute it.

One of them interrupted. "You'll still work with us, right?"

For what? They were laughing earlier at the pointlessness of our projects. But when we came up with a way to distribute our work without them, they had flashes of carrier pigeon breeders: having a job that was no longer necessary.

With the advent of this new digital age with reduced costs for creation and distribution, the possibility to create exists for everyone.

CURATION CAN WAIT

We've all heard the same arguments about an explosion of books diluting the value of the industry.

That is pure rubbish.

You are a creator, not a curator. There are people who take it upon themselves to be gatekeepers and tastemakers, whether they are book critics, movie reviewers, or your friends and family members who make recommendations.

Do you always agree with the recommendations?

Of course not.

Curation is here and in the future people will make the tech to improve it, much like the targeted ads you see when surfing the Internet.

But that's not your problem.

Your problem is making the content. Making your presence known.

Your voice matters. We need diverse books and movies. Diversity can be interpreted in different ways, but the fact is while there is only one of you, there are many others who can benefit from your perspective.

Embrace independence. We are in a better place to produce because the tools are cheaper and distribution is open and accessible.

Create your work. Worry about marketing later.

YOUR TIME IS NOW

You don't need an agent.

You don't need millions.

You just need a story.

You have lived life. You have consumed other people's stories.

Now it's your turn.

The costs have never been lower, but the stakes are only getting higher. You don't know how much time you have left, so start as soon as you possibly can.

Don't stay on the *Titanic* until a luxury cruise ship picks you up. If your idea needs a vessel, pick one that will enable you to escape ASAP. Let a book be your life preserver to Amazon. Let your cell phone camera be your lifeboat to YouTube. Put photos on Pinterest. There is room for you to make your creative escape from nonexistence to immortality. Take that golden ticket and make the voyage.

You'll have one hell of a story to tell about your trip.

FAME AND FORTUNE: FICKLE

It's all a crapshoot. If publishers with tremendous physical and financial resources knew, then all of their books would be bestsellers. It's the same for every creative industry. So we don't know if you'll get fame and fortune, but we do know this...

YOU HAVE TO BE IN IT TO WIN IT

We don't know if or when, but we know if you don't create, there will never be a when.

PRODUCE, PRODUCE, PRODUCE

It's rare to get fame from first work, but if you're in it for fame, pick another hobby. This is about something greater.

Don't keep your great work to yourself.

Put it out there and move on to the next. Adopt a visual artist production cycle. Unless the goal is creating something on commission or for a show submission, they don't stick to one painting. They're amassing work for their own exhibition.

OBSTACLES ARE CREATIVE CHALLENGES YOU CAN OVERCOME

Your path may be littered with emotional obstacles ranging from naysayers to outright haters. You might have momentum shifts like fired editors (if you go the traditional publishing route). Whether it's location, lack of capital, prohibitive production costs, or just life getting in the way, you have to continue with your vision. You can't control whether there is a market for your work. You can control your production of work. If your vision is best served by a budget you don't have, have an ideation session and tap your creative spirit. Obstacles are creative challenges that can be conquered.

YOU CAN'T PLEASE EVERYBODY

My wife and I are soul mates, but we don't have identical tastes. She bought me a book when we first met that spoke to her inner core.

It put me to sleep.

I love Charles Bukowski and *Blue Velvet*.

She hates them.

Different strokes. Does that mean there's no value in the works she likes, but only in the works I do? Not at all. So why censor ourselves?

TIME TO CREATE

First, get a recording device, whether it's an old-school notepad, smartphone, tablet, or computer. Use word-processing software or dictation software and take it with you.

- Go on a trip, whether it's a vacation or a commute.
- On your lunch break at work
- Or refuse at least one party/happy hour/activity a week and stay home to create.

Develop the habit and run with it.

HOW YOU CAN FIND THE TIME

If you can find the time to read other people's stories, you can find the time to craft your own. Eliminate some form of non-inspirational entertainment (videogames, TV, movies, music) until you finish your project. Reward yourself with it when you're done.

HOW TO MOTIVATE YOURSELF TO FOLLOW THROUGH

- Look for a book that represents you. Do you agree with everything in it?

- Look for a movie that occurs during your childhood. Are you or anyone like you represented in it?

- Read social media. Are people complaining about a movie/book/show? Do you agree? Do you disagree?

If the answer to any of the above is YES, then do something creative about it.

If not, how will future generations know you existed?

If none of these are enough, or if you need more, the next section is for you.

7 SECRET SOURCES OF INSPIRATION

The purpose of this section is to suggest the creative fuel used by some, but not all, creative professionals. It's uncertain which, if any, will work for you. I grew up in a family of thirty artists, and supervised and maintained a program that served more than 8500 individual artists and arts organizations on over 10,000 legal and business matters, and these are but a sample for collective experiences, including my own.

ONE WORD TO RULE THEM ALL

Emotion.

That is the fuel of creativity. Whether rage at injustice or love for a moment, you have emotion.

Your experience driving that emotion is special: the time it occurred will never come again. Give humanity to your traditions, cultures, and beliefs. Don't allow the media or others to do it for you. And don't waste your time with arbiters of authenticity.

You felt it. You lived it. You know what is true. You don't need to prove your credibility to a skeptical gatekeeper.

Bypass them.

Share your story to preserve your perspective. Inspire future generations.

EMOTIONAL INFLUENCERS

Unless you're inspired by boredom, chances are you need some fuel for your creativity. There are ranges of emotions you can tap for a creative kick in the butt. Some of the most powerful emotional influencers include:

Anger

Love

Hope

Fear

Excitement

Disgust

Envy

WARNING: TREAD LIGHTLY

Anger, fear, disgust, and jealousy can be dangerous motivational influences. If you choose any of these paths, you risk binging and sabotaging your creativity by wasting time wallowing in anger and frustration at the ignorance of others. It's the difference between going to a wine tasting and sampling alcohol, as opposed to binge-drinking at the pub and ending up a hot mess in an alley, soaking in your own piss and vomit.

1. SOCIAL MEDIA

ALL EMOTIONS

Social media is an exceptionally fickle muse. From personal experience, I can safely tell you that I have ended up wasting a lot of creative time gorging on the shallow stupidity of self-absorbed whining instead of producing. If you are on social media, please tread lightly lest you get caught up in an online catfight. If you are fishing for motivational fuel and read something bothersome that doesn't inspire your own creative expression, move to something else. Once you find that inspiration, don't be greedy. Reel it in, take it off the hook, put it in your boat, and oar for shore.

You have been forewarned, and, like me, will probably end up doing it anyway.

2. RESURRECT THE CLASSICS

LOVE/HATE/HOPE

Whether it's a story you love or hate, if it's in the public domain, it is yours to retell: with minor or major deviation. So many people have not been included in history. So why not fix it? Give it a fresh take by introducing an unexplored aspect of a character, whether ethnic, religious, political, or sexual orientation. Bless it with a new perspective. Make it palatable when you found it repugnant. Or make it repugnant when you found it too palatable.

Or create a new character that represents you and show the story from their point of view. She can expose the hypocrisy of the "happy slave" or the "helpless princess."

For instance, Injun Joe is one of the most damning, one-dimensional, hate-inspiring characters in modern fiction. He's an evil, angry Native American on the warpath.

And he's in the public domain.

So flesh him out. Show his side of the story. Make him more rounded. Give Native American youth who are assigned *Tom Sawyer* some hope that there is value in their ancestors. Remove the shame felt with their official literary representative. That is a true creative challenge.

You don't need to conduct a séance and get Mark Twain's permission. You can have at Injun Joe.

Or maybe there's some other character or story that really bothered you as a kid. You were forced to read in school by an unsympathetic teacher or cruel classmates. You can be sure that your experiences continue to be repeated in classrooms all over this country.

So do something about it.

Or don't, if you have other stories to tell.

3. CREATIVE VAMPIRES

ANGER/EXCITEMENT

Some of my clients have been creative vampires. They feed off the energy of others and turn it into fuel for their art.

"I hate being married to her when she has an art exhibition. She'll argue with me over anything and everything. Shout, gesture, and stomp until she goes to the basement like a troll. Slams the door and disappears for hours. When she comes back upstairs, she's back to her old self. And is giddy with her newly completed painting. I tell her that there has to be another way for motivation.

"She hasn't found it yet."

When I bar-hopped in Manhattan, I could feel the energy surrounding me. So many people. So many buildings. Electricity illuminating the city. I'd get a contact high from it, take a crowded subway ride to my small Brooklyn apartment, and spend the rest of the night writing.

Some of my clients and family members feel the same way in the boonies. The quiet, sleepy void beckons their creativity. Busy city life is a distraction.

And to a degree, I agree with them.

For many who live in the city, they talk about art, music, museums, and opera...

But rarely attend.

They're surrounded by culture and somehow feel like they're a part of something. And they are...

As a consumer.

They get too caught up in hanging out and clubbing or just working all hours of the day and night to roll up their sleeves and create. For them, being around creative people is enough. They love living vicariously. And there's nothing wrong with that.

Unless you yearn to create.

We're filled with a bunch of ideas, thoughts, emotions, longings, and yearnings. Some of us can't keep them all bottled up, so we have a creative release. We don't use sleep as a means of overcoming outrage. We don't waste time writing letters articulating our anger only to throw them away.

Instead, we create art.

You do too, but might not be aware. At times, you respond to a bad experience by making a comment. Whether it's overcooked or undercooked, under-seasoned or too spicy, you become a food critic. A coworker complains about their good-for-nothing boyfriend on Monday morning, and you become a counselor. People come to you to solve their problems, but what about your own? And are they really listening? Maybe you're too embarrassed to share. Instead of bottling up your frustration or unwittingly taking it out on innocents in the real world, and thereby losing friends and your job, why not use a creative outlet?

It's been said that humor is the angry art. Those of you with gallows humor understand what I'm talking about. Something bad happens, and you crack a joke. Not too loudly, if you don't want to offend others. Given enough time, you might be able to share the joke.

Or not.

It's that same process of fueling creativity with emotion that works for many.

Creating and consumption should be intertwined. Taking in creative projects and producing your own.

4. GARBAGE IS GOOD

DISGUST/ENVY

There are loads of suggestions for motivation. You've read a few so far in this book. Some suggest reengaging in a Spartan, monastic existence devoid of distraction.

I disagree.

I suggest you consume as much bad media as you can stomach. Visit galleries with horrid artwork. Play videogames with pointless quests. Engage is the most creatively wasteful behavior possible. And when you're at your wit's end, ask yourself one question...

"WHY NOT ME?"

Why was that junk allowed to exist? Was it that much better than the ideas you have?

There's only one way to find out.

Start creating. You might create the worst possible stinking heap of crap in the history of creativity.

And it might be your bestseller.

If not, who cares? You did something other than sit on your butt and consume.

5. LOOK AT A BESTSELLER LIST

HOPE/DISGUST/ENVY

Are you, your opinion, or people you care about represented?

Read the closest representations you can find. Something was left out.

You.

You are enabling others to control your narrative. You cannot safely assume that future generations will continue your oral history/traditions/beliefs. Ensure they get the story right instead of conducting a game of telephone.

Through creation you enable future generations to have proof of your existence and perspectives.

6. CRITICAL ACCLAIM

ENVY

Whether it is a book, movie, or piece of so-called "art," you've seen something that was supposed to be the bee's knees but ended up being a waste of time and money.

"WHY DON'T THEY HAVE STORIES ABOUT ME?"

"WHY AM I SEEING THE SAME CRAP OVER AND OVER AGAIN?"

You felt outraged and made appeals to your like-minded friends, family, and/or community members.

Then went on with your life.

And guess what? You probably ended up watching another flavor of the month and felt enraged all over again. You might have gone as far as crafting a story...

And abandoning it. Simply because life got in the way.

It doesn't have to be that way.

We're living in a time where the resources to create have never been cheaper. The means to distribute creative works have never been more accessible.

In other words, you don't have an excuse.

Stop looking for others to be your voice. End your disappointment when your creative representatives fail you and the communities they made millions pimping.

7. WATCH AN AWARDS SHOW

HOPE/ANGER/ENVY

Do this by yourself or with friends. Notice all of the stories that are missing. Watch how others are receiving accolades.

AFFIRMATIONS

Sometimes we need short reminders of why we create. Hopefully some of these will work for you. Feel free to read aloud:

- **I WAS HERE**
- **MY STORIES WILL SURVIVE ME**
- **MY DESCENDANTS WILL KNOW I LIVED**
- **FUTURE GENERATIONS WILL HAVE ACCESS TO MY KNOWLEDGE**
- **I WILL STOP SEEKING PERMISSION TO LIVE**
- **I NEED NO CORPORATE VALIDATION OF MY WORK**
- **I WILL NOT ALLOW ANYONE TO GET IN THE WAY OF MY VISION**
- **I CAN DO THIS**
- **I WILL DO THIS**
- **I WILL NOT BE STOPPED**
- **MY STORIES WILL SURVIVE MY NAYSAYERS**
- **I HAVE VALUE**
- **MY OPINIONS MATTER**
- **THERE IS VALUE TO MY EXPERIENCE**
- **MY STORIES DESERVE TO BE HEARD**
- **THERE IS AN AUDIENCE FOR MY WORK**
- **THERE ARE PEOPLE WHO SHARE MY BELIEFS**
- **I CANNOT PLEASE EVERYBODY**
- **I DO NOT WANT TO PLEASE EVERYBODY**
- **I WILL NOT BE CURATED**

STOP WAITING, START CREATING

The tools to record, distribute, and market your perspective to the masses are waiting for you.

It doesn't matter if you have the full marketing heft of a gatekeeper. From the time you publish your work until the time people discover it, they don't care who your publisher is or who you know. All they care about is whether your work speaks to them. Entertains them. Enlightens them. And guess what? The older your work, the more it represents a time that has gone forever.

But your work remains. Your voice is preserved. Your perspective is eternal.

You decide when your work is done. You have control with no filter. No one diluting your vision. No one undermining your perspective. And there is a difference between fixing typos and sterilizing your potency. Shaming you. Diluting your voice and vision. You press a button, and you are immortal.

It's self-expression in its purest form. You can present into the world.

Your voice matters. Don't die without letting the world know you were here. Without enlightening humanity. You don't know whom you will help. But that doesn't matter. You have made your life worth something. You have preserved your voice. You were here. The world is on notice. And no one can take that from you.

The cost of production is minimal.

Stop asking for permission.

Gatekeepers are no longer necessary.

Every month you delay is a month you're tempting fate.

Don't wait to create.

Let the world know who you are and what you think.

ABOUT THE AUTHOR

I grew up in a family of thirty artists, supervised and maintained a program that served more than 8500 individual artists and arts organizations on over 10,000 legal and business matters, and have authored bestselling novels and screenplays that have been selected for the Sundance Institute and the Independent Feature Project. In addition, I conduct workshops and lectures to sell-out crowds across the country. I enjoy great relationships with audiences and clients given my understanding of creative professionals, and provide solution-oriented counsel that inspires creative problem solving.

You can see samples of my work at alexeiauld.com

You can find help for your own projects at auldsolutions.com

Books by Alexei Auld

Tonto Canto Pocahontas

The Things I Prefer to be Forgotten

Billionaire Secrets of a Wanglorious Bastard

The Jerked Law Clerk

Beating in Progress

Cease to Persist

Chumped Collection

Enter Medusa

Fancy Anansi?

Picture Show Wendigo

Luscious Melchus Medley